NIGHTS AND DAYS

Books by James Merrill

POETRY

Nights and Days   *1966*
Water Street   *1962*
The Country of a Thousand Years of Peace   *1959*
First Poems   *1951*

FICTION

The (Diblos) Notebook   *1965*
The Seraglio   *1957*

NIGHTS AND DAYS

POEMS BY

JAMES MERRILL

Atheneum *New York* *1967*

The Thousand and Second Night, The Broken Home,
and *The Current* appeared first in THE NEW YORKER;
The Mad Scene and *From the Cupola,* in POETRY.
Other poems are reprinted by courtesy of THE ADAMS
HOUSE AND LOWELL HOUSE PRINTERS, THE NEW YORK REVIEW
OF BOOKS, PARTISAN REVIEW, PERSPECTIVE, QUARTERLY
REVIEW OF LITERATURE, STAND, and a souvenir program for
THE NEW YORK CITY BALLET.

Library of Congress catalog card number 66–11395
Published simultaneously in Canada by McClelland and Stewart Ltd
Manufactured in the United States of America
Composition and printing by Clarke & Way, New York
Bound by H. Wolff, New York
Designed by Harry Ford
First Printing January 1966
Second Printing March 1967
Third Printing June 1967

Contents

NIGHTS AND DAYS

Nightgown

A cold so keen,
My speech unfurls tonight
As from the chattering teeth
Of a sewing-machine.

Whom words appear to warm,
Dear heart, wear mine. Come forth
Wound in their flimsy white
And give it form.

The Thousand and Second Night

for Irma Brandeis

1. RIGOR VITAE

Istanbul. 21 March. I woke today
With an absurd complaint. The whole right half
Of my face refuses to move. I have to laugh
Watching the rest of it reel about in dismay

Under the double burden, while its twin
Sags on, though sentient, stupefied.
I'm here alone. Not quite—through fog outside
Loom wingèd letters: PAN AMERICAN.

Twenty-five hundred years this city has stood between
The passive Orient and our frantic West.
I see no reason to be depressed;
There are too many other things I haven't seen,

Like Hagia Sophia. Tea drunk, shaved and dressed . . .
Dahin! Dahin!

The house of Heavenly Wisdom first became
A mosque, is now a flame-
less void. The apse,
Militantly dislocated,
Still wears those dark-green epaulettes
On which (to the pilgrim who forgets
His Arabic) a wild script of gold whips
Has scribbled glowering, dated
Slogans: "God is my grief!" perhaps,
Or "Byzantine,
Go home!"
Above you, the great dome,

Bald of mosaic, senile, floated
In a gilt wash. Its old profusion's
Hypnotic shimmer, back and forth between
That of the abacus, that of the nebula,
Had been picked up from the floor,
The last of numberless handfuls,
By the last 18th century visitor.
You did not want to think of yourself for once,
But you had held your head erect
Too many years within such transcendental skulls
As this one not to feel the usual, if no
Longer flattering kinship. You'd let go
Learning and faith as well, you too had wrecked
Your precious sensibility. What else did you expect?

Outdoors. Uprooted, turban-crested stones
Lie side by side. It's as I might have feared.
The building, desperate for youth, has smeared
All over its original fine bones

Acres of ochre plaster. A diagram
Indicates how deep in the mudpack
The real façade is. I want *my* face back.
A pharmacist advises

The Hamam

After the hour of damp heat
One is addressed in gibberish, shown
Into a marble cell and thrown
On marble, there to be scrubbed clean,

Is wrapped in towels and a sheet
And led upstairs to this lean tomb
Made all of panes (red, amber, green)
With a glass star hung in the gloom,

Here sits effaced by gemlike moods,
Tastes neither coffee nor loukoum,
And to the attendant who intrudes

(Or archeologist or thief)
Gravely uptilts one's mask of platinum
Still dripping, in a sign of life.

And now what? Back, I guess, to the modern town.
Midway across the bridge, an infantile
Memory promises to uncramp my style.
I stop in deepening light to jot it down:

On the crest of her wrist, by the black watered silk of the
watchband, his grandmother had a wen, a hard mauve bub-
ble up from which bristled three or four white hairs. How
often he had lain in her lap and been lulled to a rhythm
easily the whole world's then—the yellowish sparkle of a
ring marking its outer limit, while in the foreground, sil-
houetted like the mosque of Suleiman the Magnificent, mass
and minarets felt by someone fallen asleep on the deck of his
moored caïque, that principal landmark's rise and fall dis-
tinguished, from any other, her beloved hand.

Cold. A wind rising. An entire city
Dissolved by rhetoric. And out there, past
The mirror of the Bosporos, what black coast
Reflecting us into immobility?

On this side, crowds, a magic-lantern beam—
Belgians on bicycles, housewives with red hair,
Masts, cries of crows blown high in the rose-blue air,
Ataturk's tailcoat . . . It is like a dream,

The "death-in-life and life-in-death" of Yeats'
Byzantium; and, if so, by the same token,
Alone in the sleepwalking scene, my flesh has woken
And sailed for the fixed shore beyond the straits.

2. THE CURE

The doctor recommended cortisone,
Diathermy, vitamins, and rest.
It worked. These months in Athens, no one's guessed
My little drama; I appear my own

Master again. However, once you've cracked
That so-called mirror of the soul,
It is not readily, if at all, made whole.
("Between the motion and the act

Falls the Shadow"—T. S. Eliot.)
Part of me has remained cold and withdrawn.
The day I went up to the Parthenon
Its humane splendor made me think *So what?*

One May noon in the Royal Park, among
The flora of l'Agneau Mystique—
Cypress, mimosa, laurel, palm—a Greek
Came up to name them for me in his tongue.

I thanked him; he thanked me, sat down. Peacocks
Trailed by, hard gray feet mashing overripe
But bitter oranges. I knew the type:
Superb, male, raucous, unclean, Orthodox

Ikon of appetite feathered to the eyes
With the electric blue of days that will
Not come again. My friend with time to kill
Asked me the price of cars in Paradise.

By which he meant my country, for in his
The stranger is a god in masquerade.
Failing to act that part, I am afraid
I was not human either—ah, who is?

He is, or was; had brothers and a wife;
Chauffeured a truck; last Friday broke his neck
Against a tree. We have no way to check
These headlong emigrations out of life.

Try, I suppose, we must, as even Valéry said,
And said more grandly than I ever shall—
Turning shut lids to the August sun, and all
Such neon figments (amber, green, and red)

Of incommunicable energy
As in my blindness wake, and at a blink
Vanish, and were the clearest hint, I think,
Of what I have been, am, and care to be.

3. CARNIVALS

Three good friends in as many months have complained,
"You were nice, James, before your trip. Or so
I thought. But you have changed. I know, I know,
People do change. Well, I'm surprised, I'm pained."

Before they disappeared into the night
Of what they said, I'd make a stab at mouthing
Promises that meant precisely nothing
And never saved my face. For they were right.

These weren't young friends, what's more. Youth would
    explain
Part of it. I have kept somewhere a page
Written at sixteen to myself at twice that age,
Whom I accuse of having become the vain

Flippant unfeeling monster I now am—
To hear them talk—and exhorting me to recall
Starlight on an evening in late fall
1943, and the walk with M.,

To die in whose presence seemed the highest good.
I met M. and his new wife last New Year's.
We rued the cold war's tainted atmospheres
From a corner table. It was understood

Our war was over. We had made our peace
With—everything. The heads of animals
Gazed in forbearance from the velvet walls.
Great drifts of damask cleaned our lips of grease.

9

Then L.—her "Let's be friends" and her clear look
Returned in disbelief. I had a herd
Of *friends*. I wanted love, if love's the word
On the foxed spine of the long-mislaid book.

A thousand and one nights! They were grotesque.
Stripping the blubber from my catch, I lit
The oil-soaked wick, then could not see by it.
Mornings, a black film lay upon the desk

. . . Where just a week ago I thought to delve
For images of those years in a Plain Cover.
Some light verse happened as I looked them over:

Postcards from Hamburg, Circa 1912

The ocelot's yawn, a sepia-dim
Shamelessness from nun's coif to spike heels,
She strokes his handlebar who kneels
To do for her what a dwarf does for him.
The properties are grim,

Are, you might want to say, unsexed
By use. A divan covered with a rug,
A flat Methusalem of Krug
Appear from tableau to tableau. The next
Shows him with muscle flexed

In resurrection from his underwear,
Gaining an underworld to harrow.
He steers her ankles like—like a wheelbarrow.
The dwarf has slipped out for a breath of air,
Leaving the monstrous pair.

10

Who are they? What does their charade convey?
Maker and Muse? Demon and Doll?
"All manners are symbolic"—Hofmannsthal.
Here's the dwarf back with cronies . . . oh I *say*!
Forget about it. They,

In time, in pain, unlearned their tricks.
Only the shrouded focusser of the lens
May still be chasing specimens
From his lone bathysphere deep in the Styx.
St. Pauli's clock struck six;

Sighing, "The death of sin is wages,"
He paid his models, bade them dress and go,
Earthlings once more, incognito
Down swarming boulevards, the contagious-
ly easy, final stages,

Dodged even by the faithful, one of whom
(Morose Great-Uncle Alastair)
Brought back these effigies and would shortly bear
Their doctrine unconfessed, we may assume,
Into his brazen tomb.

We found the postcards after her divorce,
I and Aunt Alix. She turned red with shame,
Then white, then thoughtful. "Ah, they're all the same—
Men, I mean." A pause. "Not you, of course."

And then: "We'll burn them. Light the fire." I must
Meanwhile have tucked a few into my shirt.
I spent the night rekindling with expert
Fingers—but that phase needn't be discussed. . . .

"The soul, which in infancy could not be told from the body, came with age to resemble *a body one no longer had*, whose transports went far beyond what passes, now, for sensation. All irony aside, the libertine *was* 'in search of his soul'; nightly he labored to regain those firelit lodgings. . . . Likewise, upon the Earth's mature body we inflict a wealth of gross experience—drugs, drills, bombardments—with what effect? A stale *frisson*, a waste of resources all too analogous to our own. Natural calamities (tumor and apoplexy no less than flood and volcano) may at last be hailed as positive reassurances, perverse if you like, of life in the old girl yet."

—GERMAINE NAHMAN

" . . . faced with such constant bickering, Cynthia would have to pinch herself to recall how warmly and deeply those two did, in fact, love one another."

—A. H. CLARENDON, *Psyche's Sisters*

Love. Warmth. Fist of sunlight at last
Pounding emphatic on the gulf. High wails
From your white ship: The heart prevails!
Affirm it! Simple decency rides the blast!—
Phrases that, quick to smell blood, lurk like sharks
Within a style's transparent lights and darks.

The lips part. The plume trembles. You're afloat
Upon the breathing, all-reflecting deep.
The past recedes and twinkles, falls asleep.
Fear is unworthy, say the stars by rote;
What destinations have been yours till now
Unworthy, says the leaping prow.

O skimmer of deep blue
Volumes fraught with rhyme and reason,
Once the phosphorescent meshes loosen
And the objects of your quest slip through,
Almost you can overlook a risen
Brow, a thin, black dawn on the horizon.

Except that in this virgin hemisphere
One city calls you—towers, drums, conches, bells
Tolling each year's more sumptuous farewells
To flesh. Among the dancers on the pier
Glides one figure in a suit of bones,
Whose savage grace alerts the chaperones.

He picks you out from thousands. He intends
Perhaps no mischief. Yet the dog-brown eyes
In the chalk face that stiffens as it dries
Pierce you with the eyes of those three friends.
The mask begins to melt upon your face.
A hush has fallen in the market place,

And now the long adventure

Let that wait.
I'm tired, it's late at night.

Tomorrow, if it is given me to conquer
An old distrust of imaginary scenes,
Scenes not lived through yet, the few final lines
Will lie on the page and the whole ride at anchor.

I'm home, of course. It's winter. Real
Snow fills the road. On the unmade
Brass bed lies my adored Scheherazade,
Eight-ninths asleep, tail twitching to the steel

Band of the steam heat's dissonant calypso.
The wind has died. Where would I be
If not here? There's so little left to see!
Lost friends, my long ago

Voyages, I bless you for sore
Limbs and mouth kissed, face bronzed and lined,
An earth held up, a text not wholly undermined
By fluent passages of metaphor.

4.

Now if the class will turn back to this, er,
Poem's first section—Istanbul—I shall take
What little time is left today to make
Some brief points. So. The rough pentameter

Quatrains give way, you will observe, to three
Interpolations, prose as well as verse.
Does it come through how each in turn refers
To mind, body, and soul (or memory)?

It does? Good. No, I cannot say offhand
Why this should be. I find it vaguely satis—
Yes please? The poet quotes too much? Hm. That is
One way to put it. Mightn't he have planned

For his own modest effort to be seen
Against the yardstick of the "truly great"
(In Spender's phrase)? Fearing to overstate,
He lets *them* do it—lets their words, I mean,

Enhance his—Yes, what now? Ah. How and when
Did he "affirm"? Why, constantly. And how else
But in the form. Form's what affirms. That's well
Said, if I do—[*Bells ring.*] Go, gentlemen.

5.

And when the long adventure reached its end,
I saw the Sultan in a glass, grown old,
While she, his fair wife still, her tales all told,
Smiled at him fondly. "O my dearest friend,"

Said she, "and lord and master from the first,
Release me now. Your servant would refresh
Her soul in that cold fountain which the flesh
Knows not. Grant this, for I am faint with thirst."

And he: "But it is I who am your slave.
Free me, I pray, to go in search of joys
Unembroidered by your high, soft voice,
Along that stony path the senses pave."

They wept, then tenderly embraced and went
Their ways. She and her fictions soon were one.
He slept through moonset, woke in blinding sun,
Too late to question what the tale had meant.

Maisie

1. One morning I shall find
    I have slept with your full weight upon my heart,
    Your motors and my breathing reconciled.
    The edges of the blind,

    The crack beneath the door will have blanched with day,
    The walls will be about to jar apart
    And sun to dust my lids deep in the opened flower.
    And still I shall not have sent you away.

2. When you came home without your sex
    You hid in the cupboard under the sink.
    Its gasps and gurglings must have helped somehow.

    The second noon you ventured forth,
    A silent star, furred up to tragic eyes,
    Hazarding recognition in a restaurant.

    It was horrible to see how much
    You honestly cared about food and comfort.
    The dishes refused! The chairs tried one by one!

    Eunuch and favorite both,
    You loll about, exuding that old magic
    There is mercifully no longer a market for.

3. For the good of the guest who has not yet looked over
    The roof garden's brink to the eaves just below,
    You shudder there long enough only to shriek

    (If eyes could shriek, and if they were ever
    Eyes, those chalcedony bonfires): O
    Scarpia! Avanti a Dio!
                        —then plummet from view,
    Leaving the newcomer aghast and weak.

16

The Furnished Room

Blue boughs, green fruit—
That was our wallpaper.
Two doors, both shut;
Two windows, a mirror.

Against the walls
Table and divan stood,
Odd animals,
One pine, one cherry wood.

One bore the book, the bowl,
The lamp. Its four
Legs shook. Its soul
Slid out like an empty drawer.

The other: claw-foot, soft
Belly, striped hide.
Glad in its hug we laughed.
Time howled outside.

But central heat
Hissed back and kept us warm.
Come dusk, lamplight
Lit out into a storm

Determined, all that week,
To fill us with
What no one else could wreak
On the room's myth.

A . . . face? There
It lies on the pillow by
Your turned head's tangled graying hair:
Another—like a shrunken head, too small!
My eyes in dread
Shut. Open. It is there,

Waxen, inhuman. Small.
The taut crease of the mouth shifts. It
Seems to smile,
Chin up in the wan light. Elsewhere
I have known what it was, this thing, known
The blind eye-slit

And knuckle-sharp cheekbone—
Ah. And again do.
Not a face. A hand, seen queerly. Mine.
Deliver me, I breathe
Watching it unclench with a soft moan
And reach for you.

Violent Pastoral

Against a thunderhead's
Blue marble, the eagle
Mounts with the lamb in his clutch:
Two wings, four hooves,

One pulse pounding, pounding,
So little time being given
To feel the earth shrunken,
Gong-tilt of waters,

To be at once helplessly
Aching talon and bleating
Weight, both,
Lest the pact break,

To link the rut in dust
When the rope shortens
Between foreleg and stake
With the harder spiral of making

For a nest wrapped in lightnings
And quilted with their beaks who not yet,
As with their bones who no longer,
Are wholly brothers;

Beyond Arcadia at last,
Wing, hoof, one oriented creature,
Snake-scream of pride
And bowels of fright

Lost in the rainbow, to be one
Even with the shepherd
Still looking up, who understood
And was not turned to stone.

An American Woman Explores the Estate of Friends
Who Have Fled France

for Grace

> Madame!
> And the earth opened
> As in Perrault,
> From an iron ring. I went by ladder
> After the caretaker
> Down to a buried chapel, Gallo-Roman,
> A small, groined place—
> One column, one rosette,
> One woman without features peering
> Up through the marble ripples
> Of a capsized sarcophagus . . .
> Madame!
> Like an echo,
> The second iron ring.
> Down, deeper down,
> A foot by now
> For every year of mine,
> Something remoter lay.
> Over hewn walls
> Trickled the lantern's shine.
> And on an altar, perhaps Celtic, seemed
> To stir, then stirred
> This dirt-caked, geometric—
> Heavens! A tortoise!
> Madame!
> But I stayed in the highest of spirits,
> Tried on all next day, under a flowered ceiling,
> Dresses by Alix and Chanel

My invisible hostess would not wear again.
I felt that I was steeling
Myself to bear what had to come.
Later, when that world fell,
I still could not help feeling. . . .

Time

for B. V. Winebaum

Ever that Everest
Among concepts, as prize for fruitful
Grapplings with which
The solved cross-word puzzle has now and then
Eclipsed Blake's "Sun-Flower"
(Not that one wanted a letter changed in either)
And jazz believed at seventeen
So parodied the slopes
That one mistook the mountain for a cloud . . .

Or there was blessed Patience:
Fifty-two chromosomes permitting
Trillions of 'lives'—some few
Triumphant, the majority
Blocked, doomed, yet satisfying, too,
In that with each, before starting over,
You could inquire beneath
The snowfield, the vine-monogram, the pattern
Of winged cyclists, to where the flaw lay
Crocus-clean, a trail inching between
Sheer heights and drops, and reach what might have been.

All day you had meant
To write letters, turn the key
In certain friendships, be ticked through at dusk
By hard, white, absent faces.

Let's say you went
So far as to begin: "It's me! Forgive . . . "
Too late. From the alcove came his cough,
His whimper—the old man whom sunset wakes.

Truly, could you bear another night
Keeping him company while he raved, agreeing
To Persia on horseback, just you two! when even
The garden path had been forbidden,
He was so feeble. Feeble!

He grasped your pulse in his big gray-haired hand,
Crevasses opening, numb azure. *Wait*
He breathed and glittered: *You'll regret*
You want to   Read my will first   Don't
Your old father   All he has   Be yours

Hours you raised the dark rum to his lips.
Your eyes burned. Your voice said:
"All right, we'll read Cervantes, we'll take trips.
She you loved lives. You'll see her in the morning.
You'll get well, you'll be proud of me. Don't smile!
I love you. I'll find work. You'll—I'll—"

It was light and late.
You could not remember
Sleeping. It hurt to rise.
There stood
Those features' ice-crowned, tanned—by what?—
Landmark, like yours, unwrinkled in repose.
Pouring tea strong and hot,
You swiftly wrote:

". . . this long silence. I don't know what's the matter with
me. All winter I have been trying to discipline myself—
'Empty the mind,' as they say in the handbooks, 'concentrate
upon one thing, any thing, the snowflake, the granite it falls
upon, the planet risen opposite, etc., etc.'—and failing, failing. Quicksands of leisure! Now summer's here, I *think*.

Each morning a fog rolls in from the sea. It would lift, perhaps, if you were to come and speak to it. Will you? Do! One
catches the ferry at. . . ."

The pen reels from your hand. Were you asleep?
Who were you writing to? Annette? Me? Jake?
Later, smoothing the foothills of the sheet,
You take up your worn pack.

Above their gay crusaders' dress
The monarchs' mouths are pinched and bleak.
Staggering forth in ranks of less and less
Related cards, condemned to the mystique

Of a redeeming One,
An Ace to lead them home, sword, stave, and axe,
Power, Riches, Love, a place to lay them down
In dreamless heaps, the reds, the blacks,

Old Adams and gray Eves
Escort you still. Perhaps this time . . . ?
A Queen in the discarded suit of Leaves,
Earth dims and flattens as you climb

And heaven, darkened, steams
Upon the trembling disk of tea.
Sixty or seventy more games
And you can go the rest alone maybe—

Arriving then at something not unlike
Meaning relieved of sense,
To plant a flag there on that needle peak
Whose diamond grates in the revolving silence.

Charles on Fire

Another evening we sprawled about discussing
Appearances. And it was the consensus
That while uncommon physical good looks
Continued to launch one, as before, in life
(Among its vaporous eddies and false calms),
Still, as one of us said into his beard,
"Without your intellectual and spiritual
Values, man, you are sunk." No one but squared
The shoulders of his own unloveliness.
Long-suffering Charles, having cooked and served the meal,
Now brought out little tumblers finely etched
He filled with amber liquor and then passed.
"Say," said the same young man, "in Paris, France,
They do it this way"—bounding to his feet
And touching a lit match to our host's full glass.
A blue flame, gentle, beautiful, came, went
Above the surface. In a hush that fell
We heard the vessel crack. The contents drained
As who should step down from a crystal coach.
Steward of spirits, Charles's glistening hand
All at once gloved itself in eeriness.
The moment passed. He made two quick sweeps and
Was flesh again. "It couldn't matter less,"
He said, but with a shocked, unconscious glance
Into the mirror. Finding nothing changed,
He filled a fresh glass and sank down among us.

The Art Dealer

Because I hoped to come by, when you died,
Something of yours, a virtue or a view,
I would not go to let that other you
Ask who the stranger was at your bedside.
There were days I told myself *It's sheer pretense.*
Illness indeed. Besides, who'd mind the shop?
When finally word reached me, I hung up
And sat, revolted by my ornaments.

Of course I saw you at the funeral:
Youthful, restored expertly, but a fake.
I turned aside. The fat ubiquitous Sheik
Winked from his Cadillac to have you cased
And shipped to a gold house moated with oil—
Yet one more proof of his appalling taste.

The Broken Home

Crossing the street,
I saw the parents and the child
At their window, gleaming like fruit
With evening's mild gold leaf.

In a room on the floor below,
Sunless, cooler—a brimming
Saucer of wax, marbly and dim—
I have lit what's left of my life.

I have thrown out yesterday's milk
And opened a book of maxims.
The flame quickens. The word stirs.

Tell me, tongue of fire,
That you and I are as real
At least as the people upstairs.

My father, who had flown in World War I,
Might have continued to invest his life
In cloud banks well above Wall Street and wife.
But the race was run below, and the point was to win.

Too late now, I make out in his blue gaze
(Through the smoked glass of being thirty-six)
The soul eclipsed by twin black pupils, sex
And business; time was money in those days.

Each thirteenth year he married. When he died
There were already several chilled wives
In sable orbit—rings, cars, permanent waves.
We'd felt him warming up for a green bride.

He could afford it. He was "in his prime"
At three score ten. But money was not time.

When my parents were younger this was a popular act:
A veiled woman would leap from an electric, wine-dark car
To the steps of no matter what—the Senate or the
    Ritz Bar—
And bodily, at newsreel speed, attack

No matter whom—Al Smith or José Maria Sert
Or Clemenceau—veins standing out on her throat
As she yelled *War mongerer! Pig! Give us the vote!,*
And would have to be hauled away in her hobble skirt.

What had the man done? Oh, made history.
Her business (he had implied) was giving birth,
Tending the house, mending the socks.

Always that same old story—
Father Time and Mother Earth,
A marriage on the rocks.

One afternoon, red, satyr-thighed
Michael, the Irish setter, head
Passionately lowered, led
The child I was to a shut door. Inside,

Blinds beat sun from the bed.
The green-gold room throbbed like a bruise.
Under a sheet, clad in taboos
Lay whom we sought, her hair undone, outspread,

And of a blackness found, if ever now, in old
Engravings where the acid bit.
I must have needed to touch it
Or the whiteness—was she dead?
Her eyes flew open, startled strange and cold.
The dog slumped to the floor. She reached for me. I fled.

28

Tonight they have stepped out onto the gravel.
The party is over. It's the fall
Of 1931. They love each other still.

She: Charlie, I can't stand the pace.
He: Come on, honey—why, you'll bury us all!

A lead soldier guards my windowsill:
Khaki rifle, uniform, and face.
Something in me grows heavy, silvery, pliable.

How intensely people used to feel!
Like metal poured at the close of a proletarian novel,
Refined and glowing from the crucible,
I see those two hearts, I'm afraid,
Still. Cool here in the graveyard of good and evil,
They are even so to be honored and obeyed.

. . . Obeyed, at least, inversely. Thus
I rarely buy a newspaper, or vote.
To do so, I have learned, is to invite
The tread of a stone guest within my house.

Shooting this rusted bolt, though, against him,
I trust I am no less time's child than some
Who on the heath impersonate Poor Tom
Or on the barricades risk life and limb.

Nor do I try to keep a garden, only
An avocado in a glass of water—
Roots pallid, gemmed with air. And later,

When the small gilt leaves have grown
Fleshy and green, I let them die, yes, yes,
And start another. I am earth's no less.

29

A child, a red dog roam the corridors,
Still, of the broken home. No sound. The brilliant
Rag runners halt before wide-open doors.
My old room! Its wallpaper—cream, medallioned
With pink and brown—brings back the first nightmares,
Long summer colds, and Emma, sepia-faced,
Perspiring over broth carried upstairs
Aswim with golden fats I could not taste.

The real house became a boarding-school.
Under the ballroom ceiling's allegory
Someone at last may actually be allowed
To learn something; or, from my window, cool
With the unstiflement of the entire story,
Watch a red setter stretch and sink in cloud.

Little Fanfare for Felix Magowan

Up beyond sense and praise,
There at the highest trumpet-blast
Of Fahrenheit, the sun is a great friend.
He is so brilliant and so warm!
Yet when his axle smokes and the spokes blaze
And he founders in dusk (or seems to),
Remember: he cannot change. It's earth, it's time,
Whose child you now are, quietly
Blotting him out. In the blue stare you raise
To your mother and father already the miniature,
Merciful, and lifelong eclipse,
Felix, has taken place;
The black pupil rimmed with rays
Contracted to its task—
That of revealing by obscuring
The sunlike friend behind it.
Unseen by you, may he shine back always
From what you see, from others. So welcome, friend.
Welcome to earth, time, others; to
These cool darks, of sense, of language,
Each at once thread and maze.
Finally welcome, if you like, to this
James your father's mother's father's younger son
Contrived with love for you
During your first days.

World at his feet,
Labor of generations—
No wonder the veins race.
In old Kazanjian's
Own words, "Love that carpet.
Forget the price."

Leaving the dealer's,
It was as if he had
Escaped quicksand. He
Climbed his front steps, head
High, full of dollars.
He poured the wife a brandy—

And that night not a blessed
Wink slept. The back yard
Lay senseless, bleak,
Profoundly scarred
By the moon's acid.
One after another clock

Struck midnight; one. Up through
His bare footsoles
Quicksilver shoots overcoming
The trellis of pulse
—Struck two, struck three—
Held him there, dreaming.

Kingdom reborn
In colors seen
By the hashish-eater—
Ice-pink, alizarin,
Pearl; maze shorn
Of depth; geometer

To whom all desires
Down to the last silken
Wisp o' the will
Are known: what the falcon
Sees when he soars,
What wasp and oriole

Think when they build—
And all this could
Be bargained for! Lord,
Wasn't it time you stood
On grander ground than cold
Moon-splintered board?

Thus the admired
Artifact, like clock
Or snake, struck till its poison
Was gone. Day broke,
The fever with it. Merde!
Who wanted *things*? He'd won.

Flushed on the bed's
White, lay a figure whose
Richness he sensed
Dimly. It reached him as
A cave of crimson threads
Spun by her mother against

That morning in their life
When sons with shears
Should set the pattern free
To ripple air's long floors
And bear him safe
Over a small waved sea.

The Current

Down the dawn-brown
River the charcoal woman
Swept in a boat thin
As the old moon.
White tremblings darted and broke
Under her hat's crown.
A paddle-stroke
And she was gone, in her wake
Only miniature
Whirlpools, her faint
Ritualistic cries.

Now up the stream,
Urging an unwilling
Arc of melon-rind
Painted red to match
His wares, appeared
The meat-vendor.
The young, scarred face
Under the white brim
Glowed with strain
And flamelike ripplings.
He sat in a cloud of flies.

If, further on,
Someone was waiting to thread
Morsels of beef
Onto a green
Bamboo sliver
And pose the lean brochette
Above already glowing
Embers, the river,

Flowing in one direction
By moon, by sun,
Would not be going
To let it happen yet.

Watching the Dance

1. BALANCHINE'S

Poor savage, doubting that a river flows
But for the myriad eddies made
By unseen powers twirling on their toes,

Here in this darkness it would seem
You had already died, and were afraid.
Be still. Observe the powers. Infer the stream.

2. DISCOTHÈQUE

Having survived entirely your own youth,
Last of your generation, purple gloom
Investing you, sit, Jonah, beyond speech,

And let towards the brute volume VOOM whale mouth
VAM pounding viscera VAM VOOM
A teenage plankton luminously twitch.

The Mad Scene

Again last night I dreamed the dream called Laundry.
In it, the sheets and towels of a life we were going to share,
The milk-stiff bibs, the shroud, each rag to be ever
Trampled or soiled, bled on or groped for blindly,
Came swooning out of an enormous willow hamper
Onto moon-marbly boards. We had just met. I watched
From outer darkness. I had dressed myself in clothes
Of a new fiber that never stains or wrinkles, never
Wears thin. The opera house sparkled with tiers
And tiers of eyes, like mine enlarged by belladonna,
Trained inward. There I saw the cloud-clot, gust by gust,
Form, and the lightning bite, and the roan mane unloosen.
Fingers were running in panic over the flute's nine gates.
Why did I flinch? I loved you. And in the downpour laughed
To have us wrung white, gnarled together, one
Topmost mordent of wisteria,
As the lean tree burst into grief.

From the Cupola

for H.M.

The sister who told fortunes prophesied
A love-letter. In the next mail it came.
You didn't recognize the writer's name
And wondered he knew yours. Ah well. That seed

Has since become a world of blossom and bark.
The letters fill a drawer, the gifts a room.
No hollow of your day is hidden from
His warm concern. Still you are in the dark.

Too much understanding petrifies.
The early letters struck you as blackmail.
You have them now by heart, a rosy veil
Colors the phrase repaired to with shut eyes.

Was the time always wrong for you to meet?—
Not that he ever once proposed as much.
Your sisters joke about it. "It's too rich!
Somebody Up There loves you, Psyche sweet."

Tell me about him, then. Not a believer,
I'll hold my tongue while you, my dear, dictate.
Him I have known too little (or, of late,
Too well) to trust my own view of your lover.

Oh but one has many, many tongues!
And you will need a certain smouldering five
Deep in the ash of something I survive,
Poke and rummage with as reluctant tongs

As possible. The point won't be to stage
One of our torchlit hunts for truth. Truth asks
Just this once to sleep with fiction, masks
Of tears and laughter on the moonstruck page;

To cauterize what babbles to be healed—
Just this once not by candor. Here and now,
Psyche, I quench that iron lest it outglow
A hovering radiance your fingers shield.

Renaissance features grafted onto Greek
Revival, glassed, hexagonal lookouts crown
Some of the finest houses in this town.
By day or night, cloud, sunbeam, lunatic streak,

They alternately ravish and disown
Earth, sky, and water—Are you with me? Speak.

SUNLIGHT   Crossfire
of rays and shadows each
glancing off a windowpane a stone
You alone my correspondent

have remained sheer
projection   Hurt   Not gravely   Not at all
Your bloodlessness a glaze
of thin thin varnish where I kneel

Were the warm drop
upon your letter oil and were that page
your sleeping person then
all would indeed be lost

Our town is small
its houses built like temples
The rare stranger I let pass with lowered
eyes   He also could be you

Nights the last red
wiped from my lips the harbor
blinking out gem by gem how utterly
we've been undressed

You will not come
to the porch at noon will you rustling your wings
or masked as crone or youth
The mouths behind our faces kiss

Kindlings of truth
Risen from the dawn mist
some wriggling silver in a tern's beak scrawls
joyous memoranda onto things

TODAY I have your letter from the South
where as a child I   but of course you know
Three times I've read it at my attic window
A city named for palms half mummy and half myth
pools flashing talking birds the world of my
first vision of you Psyche   Though it's May

that could be frost upon the apple trees
silvery plump as sponges above the pale
arm of the Sound and the pane is chill to feel
I live now by the seasons burn and freeze
far from that world where nothing changed or died
unless to be reborn on the next tide

You daylong in the saddles of foaming opal
ride   I am glad   Come dusk lime juice and gin
deepen the sunset under your salt skin
I've tasted that side of the apple
A city named for palms half desert and half dream
its dry gold settles on my mouth   I bloom

Where nothing died   Breaking on us like waves
the bougainvillea bloomed fell bloomed again
The new sea wall rose from the hurricane
and no less staunchly from the old freed slave's
ashes each night her grandchild climbed the stairs
to twitch white gauze across the stinging stars

City half dream half desert where at dawn
the sprinkler dervish whirled and all was crystalline
within each house half brothel and half shrine
up from the mirror tabletop had flown
by noon the shadow of each plate each spoon to float
in light that warbled on the ceiling   Wait

ALICE has entered talking

Any mirage if seen from a remote stand
point is refreshing   Yes but dust and heat
lie at its heart   Poor Psyche you forget
That was a cruel impossible wonderland

The very sidewalks suffered   Ours that used
to lead can you remember to the beach
I felt it knew and waited for us each
morning to trot its length in teardrop punctured shoes

when in fact the poor dumb thing lay I now know
under a dark spell cast from quite another
quarter the shadow of a towering mother
smooth as stone and thousandbreasted though

her milk was watery scant so much for love
false like everything in that whole world
However   This shadow that a royal palm hurled
onto the sidewalk from ten yards above

41

day night rustling and wrestling never shattered
except to mend back forth or lost its grip
the batwing offspring of her ladyship
Our orchid stucco house looked on greenshuttered

stoic   But the sidewalk suffered most
Like somebody I shall not name it lacked
perspective   It failed absolutely to detect
the root of all that evil   The clues it missed

Nights after a windstorm great yellow paper
dry branches lying on the curb in heaps
like fancy dress don't ask me whose someone who steps
forth and is changed by the harsh moonlight to vapor

the sidewalk could only grit itself and shift
Some mornings respite   A grisaille opaque
as poured concrete   And yet by ten o'clock
the phantom struck again in a first sunshaft

Off to the beach   Us nurse in single file
Those days we'd meet our neighbor veiled and hatted
tanagra leading home out of the sun she hated
a little boy with water wings   We'd smile

then hold our breaths to pass a barricade
of black smells rippling up from the soft hot
brink of the mirage past which sidewalks could not
follow   Ours stood there crumbling then obeyed

a whisper back of it and turned   The sea the loose
unshadowed sand too free white heterodox
ever to be congealed into sidewalks
ours never saw   GIVE ME THE SNAPPED SHOELACE

LIZARDS ANTS SCRAPS OF SILVER FOIL
hoarse green tongues begged from each new crack   No use
The shadow trod it as our nightmares us
Then we moved here where gray skies are the rule

What   Why not simply have cut down the tree
Psyche I can't believe my   Hush   You child
Cut down the   I've got gooseflesh   Feel   I'm chilled
My sister's hyperthyroid eyes fix me

The whites lackluster shot with miniature
red brambles abruptly glitter overspill
down powdered cheeks   Alice can weep at will
How to convey the things I feel for her

She is more strange than Iceland bathed all night
an invalid in sunshine   Lava cliffs
The geyser that erupts the loon that laughs
I move to kiss her but she hums a note

and licks her lips   *Well darling I must fly*
before you read what it does not intend
about yourself and your mysterious friend
say or some weird rivalry that I

may once have harbored though I harbor none
now nor does Gertrude not the tiniest pang
into this long but kindly meant harangue
She nods and leaves the room   And I am here alone

I place the ladder hoist from rung to rung
my pail and cloths into a cupola glassed
entirely with panes some tinted amethyst
it is my task to clean   Up here among

spatterings and reflections wipe as I will
these six horizons still the rain's dry ghost
and my own features haunt the roofs the coast
How does one get to know a landscape well

When did we leave the South   Why do we live indoors
I wonder sweating to the cadence   Even
on sunless days the cupola is an oven
Views blur   This thing we see them through endures

MIDNIGHT   I dream I dream   The slow moon eludes
one stilled cloud   Din of shimmerings   From across the
      Sound
what may have begun as no more
than a willow's sleepwalking outline quickens detaches
comes to itself in the cupola
panics from pane to pane and then impulsively
surrendering fluttering by now the sixteenfold
wings of the cherubim unclipped by faith or reason
stands there my dream made whole
over whose walls again
a red vine black in moonlight crawls
made habitable   Each cell of the concrete
fills with sweet light   The wave breaks
into tears   Come if its you   Step down
to where I   Stop   For at your touch the dream

cracks the angel tenses flees

NOON finds me faced by a small troop of furies
They are my senses shrill and ominous
We who were trained they cry *to do your pleasure
are kept like children   Is this fair to us*

44

Dear ones I say bending to kiss their faces
trust me   One day you'll understand   Meanwhile
suppose we think of things to raise our spirits
and leading the two easiest to beguile

into the kitchen feed them shots of Bourbon
Their brother who loves Brahms conceives a wish
for gems from L'Africana played at volumes
that make the dwarf palm shudder in its dish

The pale one with your eyes restively flashing
takes in the dock the ashen Sound the sky
The fingers of the eldest brush my features
But you are smiling she says coldly   *Why*

     STAR or candle being lit
          but to shed itself
       into blackness partly night's
sure that no less golden warm than it
          is our love
       will have missed the truth by half
     We see according to our lights

     Eros   husband   names distort
         you who have no name
     Peace upon your neophytes
Help me when the christenings shall start
         o my love
     to defend your sleep from them
     and see according to our lights

Ah and should discernment's twin
            tyrants adamant
for their meal of pinks and whites
be who call those various torches in
                help me love
      This is nothing I shall want
      We see according to our lights

When as written you have lapsed
            back into the god
darts and wings and appetites
what of him the lover all eclipsed
            by sheer love
      Shut my eyes it does no good
      Who will ever put to rights

Psyche, hush. This is me, James,
            Writing lest he think
Of the reasons why he writes—
Boredom, fear, mixed vanities and shames;
            Also love.
      From my phosphorescent ink
      Trickle faint unworldly lights

Down your face. Come, we'll both rest.
            Weeping? You must not.
All our pyrotechnic flights
Miss the sleeper in the pitch-dark breast.
            He is love:
      He is everyone's blind spot.
      We see according to our lights.

"What's that sound? Is it you, dear?"

"Yes. I was just eating something."

"What?"

"I don't know—I mean, an apricot . . ."

"Hadn't you best switch on the light and make sure?"

"No, thank you, Gertrude."

A hurt silence ensued.

"Oh, Psyche!" her sister burst out at length. "Here you are, surrounded by loving kin, in a house crammed with lovely old things, and what do you crave but the unfamiliar, the 'transcendental'? I declare, you're turning into the classic New England old maid!"

.   .   .   .

Psyche's hands dropped from her wet, white face. The time had come—except that Time, like Love, wears a mask in this story, whose action requires perhaps thirty-six hours of Spring, perhaps thirty-six Springs of a life—a moment nevertheless had come to take the electric torch and leave her sisters without a word. Later she was to recall a tear-streaked muzzle, the marvelous lashed golds of an iris reflecting her own person backed by ever tinier worlds of moonlight and tossing palms, then, at the center, blackness, a fixed point, a spindle on which everything had begun to turn. Piercing her to the brain.

Spelt out in brutal prose, all had been plain.

RAIN   Evening   The drive in   My sisters' gold sedan's
     eyes have gone dim and dark   windows are sealed
          For vision's sake two wipers wield
     the automatic coquetry of fans

47

In the next car young Eros and his sweetheart sit
    fire and saltwater still from their embrace
        Grief plays upon his sated face
    Her mask of tears does not exactly fit

The love goddess his mother overflows a screen
    sixty feet wide or seems to   Who can plumb
        those motes of rose and platinum
    At once they melt back into the machine

throbbing dry and dispassionate beyond our ken
    to spool her home whose beauty flabbergasts
        The nervous systems of her guests
    drink and drink the sparkling staleness in

Now in her element steam she looms up from a bath
    The hero's breastplate mirrors her red lips
        It burns and clouds   As waterdrops
    course down the monumental cheeks of both

they kiss   My sisters turn on me from either side
    shrieking with glee under the rainlight mask
        fondle and pinch in mean burlesque
    of things my angel you and I once tried

In no time he alone is left of a proud corps
    That dustcloud hides triumphant fleeing Huns
        Lips parched by a montage of suns
    he cannot taste our latter night's downpour

while she by now my sisters fatten upon fact
    is on location in Djakarta where
        tomorrow's sun illumines her
    emoting in strange arms   It's all an act

48

Eros are you like her so false a naked glance
    turns you into that slackjawed fleshproud youth
        driving away   Was he your truth
    Is it too late to study ignorance

These fictive lives these loves of the comedian
    so like so unlike ours which hurt and heal
        are what the gods know   You can feel
    lust and fulfillment Eros no more than

ocean its salt depths or uranium its hot
    disintegrative force or I our fable
        My interest like the rain grown feeble
    a film of sorrow on my eyes they shut

I may already be part god   Asleep awake
    some afterglow as of a buried heaven
        keeps flickering through me   I may even
    learn to love it Eros for your sake

MORNING   The task is done   When my sisters wake
they will look once more upon pale water and clear sky
a fair far brow of land
with its fillet of Greek trees oak apple willow
and here below in the foreground
across a street finished down to the last detail
a red clapboard temple   The neat outlines
it's a warehouse really have been filled with colors
dull red flaking walls   white trim
and pediment   tar roof patched black on black
Greek colors   An effect I hope
not too much spoiled by a big yellow legend
BOAT WORKS on the roof which seagulls helicopters

49

the highup living and the happy dead
are in a position to read
Outside indeed a boat lies covered with tarpaulin
Old headlines mend a missing pane   The warehouse
seems but in the time it takes to say *abandoned*
a face male old molepale in sun
though blinded by the mullion's shadow
has floated to an eerie scale the rising
wind flutes out of the oaken depths
I look away   When I look back
the panic's over   It is afternoon
Now the window reflects my sisters' white
mock Ionic portico and me emerging
blinking   Too bright to bear or turn from
spring's first real sun burns on the numb blue Sound
Beyond the warehouse past the round GULF sign
whose warning it ignores a baby dock has waded
The small waves stretch their necks gulls veer and scold
I walk the length of our Greek Revival village
from library to old blind lighthouse
Like one entranced who talks as awake she cannot
a potpourri of dead chalkpetal dialects
dead anyhow all winter
lips caulked with faded pollen and dust of cloves
I find that I can break the cipher
come to light along certain humming branches
make out not only *apple blossom* and *sun*
but perfectly the dance of darker undertones
on pavement or white wall   It is this dance I know
that cracks the pavement   I do know
Finally I reach a garden where I am to uproot
the last parsnips for my sisters' dinner

Not parsnips mastodons   But this year's greens
already frill them and they pull easily
from the soft ground   Two of the finest
are tightly interlocked have grown that way   They lie
united in the grave of sunny air
as in their breathing living dark
I look at them a long while
mealy and soiled in one another's arms
and blind full to the ivory marrow
with tender blindness   Then I bury them
once more in memory of us
Back home   Gold skies   My basket full
Lifting it indoors I turn   The little dock
It is out there still on stilts in freezing water
It must know by now
that no one is coming after it that it must wait
for morning for next week for summer
by which time it will have silvered and splintered
and the whitewinged boats and the bridegroom's burning
        sandals
will come too late   It's dark   It's dinner time
Light the lamp my sisters call from where they eat
There follows a hushed preening and straining
wallpaper horsehair glass wood pewter glue
Now is their moment when all else goes black
and what is there but substance to turn to
Sister the lamp   The round
moon mallet has risen and struck   Of the warehouse
        pulverized
one faintest blueprint glimmers by which to build it
on the same spot tomorrow somehow right
Light your lamp Psyche dear

My hand is on the switch I have done this
faithfully each night since the first
Tonight I think will not be different
Then soft light lights the room the furniture
a blush invades even the dropped lid
yes and I am here alone
I and my flesh and blood

Thank you, Psyche. I should think those panes
Were just about as clear as they can be.
It's time I turned my light on. Child, leave me.
Here on the earth we loved alone remains

One shrunken amphitheatre, look, to moon
Hugely above. Ranked glintings from within
Hint that a small articulate crowd has been
Gathered for days now, waiting. None too soon,

Whether in lower or in upper case,
Will come the Moment for the metal of each
To sally forth—once more into the breach!
Beyond it, glory lies, a virgin space

Acrackle in white hunger for the word.
We've seen what comes next. There is no pure deed.
A black-and-red enchanter, a deep-dyed
Coil of—No matter. One falls back, soiled, blurred.

And on the page, of course, black only. Damned
If I don't tire of the dark view of things.
I think of your 'Greek colors' and it rings
A sweet bell. Time to live! Haven't I dimmed

That portion of the ribbon—whose red glows
Bright with disuse—sufficiently for a bit?
Tomorrow mayn't I start to pay my debt,
In wine, in heart's blood, to la vie en rose?

This evening it will do to be alone,
Here, with your girlish figures: parsnip, Eros,
Shadow, blossom, windowpane. The warehouse.
The lamp I smell in every other line.

Do you smell mine? From its rubbed brass a moth
Hurtles in motes and tatters of itself
—Be careful, tiny sister, drabbest sylph!—
Against the hot glare, the consuming myth,

Drops, and is still. My hands move. An intense,
Slow-paced, erratic dance goes on below.
I have received from whom I do not know
These letters. Show me, light, if they make sense.

Days of 1964

Houses, an embassy, the hospital,
Our neighborhood sun-cured if trembling still
In pools of the night's rain . . .
Across the street that led to the center of town
A steep hill kept one company part way
Or could be climbed in twenty minutes
For some literally breathtaking views,
Framed by umbrella pines, of city and sea.
Underfoot, cyclamen, autumn crocus grew
Spangled as with fine sweat among the relics
Of good times had by all. If not Olympus,
An out-of-earshot, year-round hillside revel.

I brought home flowers from my climbs.
Kyria Kleo who cleaned for us
Put them in water, sighing *Virgin, Virgin.*
Her legs hurt. She wore brown, was fat, past fifty,
And looked like a Palmyra matron
Copied in lard and horsehair. How she loved
You, me, loved us all, the bird, the cat!
I think now she *was* love. She sighed and glistened
All day with it, or pain, or both.
(We did not notably communicate.)
She lived nearby with her pious mother
And wastrel son. She called me her real son.

I paid her generously, I dare say.
Love makes one generous. Look at us. We'd known
Each other so briefly that instead of sleeping
We lay whole nights, open, in the lamplight,
And gazed, or traded stories.

One hour comes back—you gasping in my arms
With love, or laughter, or both,
I having just remembered and told you
What I'd looked up to see on my way downtown at noon:
Poor old Kleo, her aching legs,
Trudging into the pines. I called,
Called three times before she turned.
Above a tight, skyblue sweater, her face
Was painted. Yes. Her face was painted
Clown-white, white of the moon by daylight,
Lidded with pearl, mouth a poinsettia leaf,
Eat me, pay me—the erotic mask
Worn the world over by illusion
To weddings of itself and simple need.

Startled mute, we had stared—was love illusion?—
And gone our ways. Next, I was crossing a square
In which a moveable outdoor market's
Vegetables, chickens, pottery kept materializing
Through a dream-press of hagglers each at heart
Leery lest he be taken, plucked,
The bird, the flower of that November mildness,
Self lost up soft clay paths, or found, foothold,
Where the bud throbs awake
The better to be nipped, self on its knees in mud—
Here I stopped cold, for both our sakes;

And calmer on my way home bought us fruit.

Forgive me if you read this. (And may Kyria Kleo,
Should someone ever put it into Greek
And read it aloud to her, forgive me, too.)
I had gone so long without loving,
I hardly knew what I was thinking.

Where I hid my face, your touch, quick, merciful,
Blindfolded me. A god breathed from my lips.
If that was illusion, I wanted it to last long;
To dwell, for its daily pittance, with us there,
Cleaning and watering, sighing with love or pain.
I hoped it would climb when it needed to the heights
Even of degradation, as I for one
Seemed, those days, to be always climbing
Into a world of wild
Flowers, feasting, tears—or was I falling, legs
Buckling, heights, depths,
Into a pool of each night's rain?
But you were everywhere beside me, masked,
As who was not, in laughter, pain, and love.

James Merrill

James Merrill was born in New York in 1926.
He lives in Stonington, Connecticut. He is the author
of three earlier books of poems: *Water Street* (1962),
The Country of a Thousand Years of Peace (1959),
and *First Poems* (1951); two novels: *The (Diblos)
Notebook* (1965), and *The Seraglio* (1957); and two
plays: *The Immortal Husband* (given an off-Broadway
production in 1955 and published the following year
in PLAYBOOK) and, in one act, *The Bait*,
published in ARTIST'S THEATRE (1960).